THE LIBRARY OF AMERICAN LAWS AND LEGAL PRINCIPLES ™

THE CIVIL RIGHTS ACT OF 1964

Landmark Antidiscrimination Legislation

Susan Wright

The Rosen Publishing Group, Inc., New York

Published in 2006 by The Rosen Publishing Group, Inc.
29 East 21st Street, New York, NY 10010

First Edition

Library of Congress Cataloging-in-Publication Data

Wright, Susan, 1939–
The Civil Rights Act of 1964: landmark antidiscrimination legislation/by Susan Wright.–1st ed.
    p. cm.–(The library of American laws and legal principles)
Includes bibliographical references and index.
ISBN 1-4042-0455-5 (library binding)
1. United States. Civil Rights Act of 1964–Juvenile literature. 2. Civil rights–United States–History–20th century–Juvenile literature. I. Title. II. Series.
KF4744.5151964.W75 2006
342.7308'5'09046–dc22
                                                                                    2005007295

Manufactured in the United States of America

On the cover: The main entrance of the United States Supreme Court building faces the U.S. Capitol in Washington, D.C. The marble statue on the right side of the entrance represents Authority of Law and was carved by James Earle Fraser. The male figure holds a sword and a tablet, on which is written the Latin word *Lex*, meaning "law."

CONTENTS

INTRODUCTION

Before the historic Civil Rights Act of 1964, African Americans in the South couldn't go into most public swimming pools, parks, or libraries. Segregation meant that African Americans weren't allowed in certain schools, restaurants, motels, and theaters. African Americans had to sit in separate areas on buses and in waiting rooms. Signs even marked the water fountains and restrooms they could use. Most black adults couldn't vote, so they had no voice in government. Most had to work as poorly paid maids or laborers.

Even worse was the violence African Americans faced in the South. Emmett Till, a fourteen-year-old boy from Chicago, was visiting relatives in Mississippi in the summer of 1955, when he was murdered by two white men. Till had whistled at a young white woman and called her "babe." For this, he was brutally beaten and thrown in the Tallahatchie River. In the trial that followed, the murderers were found not guilty by the all-white, all-male jury. Many white people in the South thought it was justifiable to kill a black man for doing what Till did.

The civil rights movement of the 1950s and 1960s was organized to protest the unfair treatment of black Americans. A growing unrest was spreading through the country in response to racial discrimination and the segregation of all racial minorities.

In 1963, the leaders of the civil rights movement chose Birmingham, Alabama, for a major series of peaceful demonstrations, marches, boycotts, and sit-ins. The world was shocked when television images

This photograph of Emmett Till was taken in 1955, the year he was killed for flirting with a white woman. His death and the acquittal of the men who murdered him mobilized the civil rights movement and set off an international firestorm protesting the mistreatment of African Americans and other racial minorities in the United States.

showed the police driving out demonstrators with powerful fire hoses that sent them tumbling down the street. Demonstrators were beaten, and law enforcement officers used German shepherds to attack them. Many of the protesters–including children–were arrested.

Many Americans couldn't ignore these terrible images, and they felt that it was time to address the problem of discrimination in American society. Rising to the challenge, President John F. Kennedy addressed the nation on June 11, 1963, saying:

> *We are confronted primarily with a moral issue. It is as old as the scriptures and it is as clear as the American Constitution. The heart of the question is whether all Americans are afforded equal rights and equal opportunities, whether we are going to treat our fellow Americans as we want to be treated.*

President Kennedy created a strong civil rights bill to end segregation and discrimination. However, getting it passed would be difficult. Opposition from Southern congressmen had kept legislation like this from being passed before.

By the end of the summer, a groundswell of support for civil rights led to the first March on Washington. Nearly 250,000 people surrounded the Lincoln Memorial on August 28, 1963. Eighty million television viewers watched as Martin Luther King Jr., the recognized leader of the civil rights movement, declared in his famous "I have a dream" speech:

> *Even though we face the difficulties of today and tomorrow, I still have a dream. It is a dream deeply rooted in the American dream. I have a dream that one day this nation will rise up and live out the true meaning of its creed, "We hold these Truths to be self-evident, that all Men are created equal."*

Later that day, the leaders of the march met with President Kennedy at the White House. Kennedy praised "the deep fervor and quiet dignity of the marchers." But Kennedy did not live to see his civil rights bill become law. He was shot and killed by an assassin in November 1963, in Dallas, Texas.

Kennedy's successor was Lyndon B. Johnson. Johnson had helped create the Civil Rights Act of 1957, but it was a very weak bill. It created the Civil Rights Division under the attorney general of the United States, but there were only ten lawyers to investigate complaints.

Though Johnson was a Southerner—a Texan—he supported Kennedy's civil rights bill. He had been born in a poverty-stricken region and had attended a one-room schoolhouse when he was growing up. Johnson had seen for himself how segregation prevented minorities from bettering their lives.

Dr. Martin Luther King Jr. waves to the throng of demonstrators during the March on Washington on August 28, 1963. The event was the largest political demonstration in American history to that date. Because of the sheer size of the crowd and King's powerful "I have a dream" address, it was one of the most pivotal moments in the African American struggle for civil rights.

Five days after Kennedy's assassination, President Johnson eloquently addressed a joint session of Congress. He said:

We have talked long enough in this country about civil rights. It is time to write the next chapter and to write it in the books of law . . . No eulogy could more eloquently honor President Kennedy's memory than the earliest possible passage of the civil rights bill for which he fought so long.

Johnson worked closely with civil rights leaders to convince members of Congress and senators to vote for the bill. There were many compromises made to ensure the Civil Rights Act was approved. One of these compromises had profound implications for women's rights.

At the last minute, Congressman Howard Smith of Virginia, who opposed the civil rights legislation, added an amendment prohibiting discrimination in the workplace based on sex. Smith thought that Congress would reject a bill that required equal rights for women. Some supporters of civil rights fought this amendment, fearing it would doom the bill.

However, female members of Congress spoke out about the need to provide equal job opportunities for women. Congresswoman Katherine St. George of New York argued that she could think of "nothing more logical than this amendment" and that "we are entitled to this little crumb of equality," as quoted on the official Equal Employment Opportunity Commission's Web site.

On February 10, 1964, the House of Representatives passed the measure by a 290 to 130 vote. However, the real fight was in the Senate, where the rules allow senators to filibuster—speaking merely to waste time—thereby preventing a vote on a bill. In this way, many Southerners had prevented a number of earlier civil rights bills from being passed.

But it was clearly time for a change in America. The most important piece of civil rights legislation in American history was approved by the Senate. On July 2, President Johnson signed the Civil Rights Act of 1964 into law.

CHAPTER ONE

The Need for the Civil Rights Act of 1964

T he Declaration of Independence, signed on July 4, 1776, reads, "We hold these Truths to be self-evident, that all Men are created equal." Despite this proud proclamation, the Founding Fathers decided that people of African heritage could be enslaved. In the century that passed until the Civil War (1861–1865), slavery became the backbone of the plantation economy in the South. Slave labor produced cotton for Northern factories. Even after President Abraham Lincoln issued the Emancipation Proclamation in 1863, freeing the slaves in the South, serious problems of racial discrimination and segregation remained for America's minorities.

Basic human rights and respect were given to white males, while minorities were persecuted. Blacks were often not allowed to vote. Women were paid less than men for doing the same job. Some businesses and public organizations catered to white Protestants only, excluding Catholics. People with disabilities could not get jobs. The fundamental idea of democracy—that the government is for, by, and of the people—was largely ignored in practice.

JIM CROW

After the Civil War, three amendments to the U.S. Constitution were added to ensure freedom and equality for all people in the United States. The Thirteenth Amendment (1865) abolished slavery everywhere in the United States. The Fourteenth Amendment (1868) established that all people born in the United States were citizens, thereby giving them equal protection under the law. The Fifteenth Amendment (1869) gave all citizens the right to vote.

Despite the promises of these new laws, the former slaves and their descendants, along with other minorities, did not receive equal treatment. The history of slavery in the United States meant that black people were dehumanized; they were considered to be and treated as if they were less than human.

Southern states passed their own laws, which denied black people their rights and kept them away from white people. Some of these laws prevented blacks from owning or renting farms. Others decreed that black people could work only on plantations or as servants. African Americans could even be arrested for "uppity behavior"—standing up for themselves. The laws of this discriminatory system became known as the Jim Crow laws.

In 1892, an African American man named Homer Plessy was arrested for riding in the white section of a train in Louisiana. Plessy believed he had the right to ride in any railroad car because the Fourteenth Amendment states, "No state shall . . . abridge the privileges . . . of citizens of the United States." It seemed clear that keeping people separate on a train abridged, or limited, black people's rights.

Nevertheless, in 1896, the U.S. Supreme Court ruled that state governments could separate people of different races as long as the separate facilities were equal. This "separate but equal" doctrine lasted until 1954. Justice Henry Billings Brown wrote the Court's decision, which said that the Fourteenth Amendment "could not have been intended to abolish distinctions based upon color, or to enforce social . . . equality, or a commingling of the two races." Only one of the Supreme Court justices, John Marshall Harlan, disagreed with the decision.

As announced by the sign on the building, this cinema in Leland, Mississippi, was segregated under Jim Crow laws in 1939, when the photograph was taken. Signs such as this were all over the South during segregation. Even when no signs were posted, blacks were expected to know—and they knew—the places that were off-limits to them.

Throughout the country, it was quite obvious that the services offered for "whites only" were much better than those offered for "Negroes." Every public place was segregated in the South—schools, restaurants, hotels, even phone booths. The nation's favorite sport, baseball, had the major leagues, the minor leagues, and the Negro leagues for black ballplayers.

Other ethnic groups were also targeted for discrimination. For example, Jim Crow laws also barred Chinese students from attending public schools. In 1924, a Chinese grocer, Gong Lum, filed a lawsuit when his daughter was refused admission to a "whites-only" school in Mississippi. The case went to the Supreme Court, which upheld

Mississippi's right "to preserve the white schools for members of the Caucasian race alone."

Although Congress finally granted citizenship to all Native Americans in 1924, that didn't end their segregation. A reporter who visited Alaska in 1943 said that the social position of Native Americans and Inuits was "equivalent to that of a Negro in Georgia or Mississippi," as quoted in *All the People* by Joy Hakim.

Discrimination was so widespread that it even applied to soldiers at war. During World War II (1939–1945), minority soldiers were formed into separate units and were often given the dirtiest, most dangerous jobs. They weren't allowed to serve alongside white men, but they died to preserve American freedoms just the same. In Mississippi, when some black soldiers returned home, they were dumped from army trucks and beaten.

Between 1940 and 1970, 5 million African Americans moved from the South to the North to escape Jim Crow laws. But prejudice and separation was rampant in the North as well, even though there was less legal segregation. Schools were (and still are) mostly attended by children of the same race because neighborhoods were racially divided. Real estate agents used to refuse to show black people homes in white neighborhoods. Most blacks were forced to live in the poorest neighborhoods, where the services, streets, and buildings were substandard.

President Harry S. Truman, who was in office from 1945 to 1953, had been brought up in the South, so he had seen prejudice himself. Truman sent proposals to Congress to end segregation in the armed services; to outlaw the poll tax, which kept poor blacks from voting; and to stop lynchings—public murders that were racially motivated. Sadly, Congress refused most of Truman's proposals.

CIVIL RIGHTS MOVEMENT

Organized in 1909, the National Association for the Advancement of Colored People (NAACP) is the oldest civil rights organization in the United States. In the 1930s, Charles Houston and Thurgood Marshall, two African American lawyers, documented the shacks and log cabins that black children had to use for schools and compared them to the modern, well-equipped schools attended by white children in the same towns. After World War II, the NAACP sued for equal school facilities and won.

But school facilities still weren't equal. In South Carolina's Clarendon County, $43 a year was spent on each black student while $179 was spent on each white student. Two of the black schools had no desks for the students.

So in 1952, Marshall took on the case of a seven-year-old girl named Linda Brown. She lived in Topeka, Kansas, and had to attend a black school that was far from her home. To get there, she had to cross railroad tracks and ride a long way in an old school bus, even though there was a white school five blocks from her home.

The Supreme Court decided the case on school segregation on May 17, 1954, in what became known as *Brown v. Board of Education.* It ruled that segregation in the public schools was a violation of the Fourteenth Amendment to the Constitution. Chief Justice Earl Warren stated in the decision: "We conclude, unanimously, that in the field of public education the doctrine of 'separate but equal' has no place. Separate educational facilities are inherently unequal."

According to the Court's order, desegregation was supposed to happen "with all deliberate speed." In some places, schools were integrated without any problems. But in others, black children were insulted, spat on, and hit with rocks.

Southern states passed more than 450 laws to stop or slow down school integration. James O. Eastland, a U.S. senator from Mississippi, declared, "On May 17, 1954, the Constitution of the United States was destroyed because of the Supreme Court's decision. You are not obligated to obey the decisions of any court which are plainly fraudulent," as quoted in *Getting Away with Murder* by Chris Crowe.

In the landmark Supreme Court case of *Brown v. Board of Education*, the NAACP showed that the crowded, ill-equipped classrooms assigned to African American communities *(top)* were markedly inferior to "white-only" schools, and that segregation was unconstitutional. Three of the prosecuting lawyers *(bottom left, left to right)*, George Hayes, Thurgood Marshall, and James Nabrit, celebrated the ruling in front of the Supreme Court building on May 17, 1954. The school at the center of the case, Monroe Elementary School *(bottom right)*, is now a national historic site.

Keeping Kids Out of School

In 1957, a federal court ordered the desegregation of public schools in Little Rock, Arkansas. The governor of Arkansas, Orval Faubus, ordered the Arkansas National Guard to prevent nine black children from entering the all-white Central High School in Little Rock. To gain control, President Eisenhower annexed the National Guard as part of the federal army. The president also sent 1,000 paratroopers to protect the children. In September 1958, Governor Faubus closed all the schools in Little Rock to prevent school integration. The schools remained closed until August 1959, when the U.S. Supreme Court ordered them reopened.

With the Supreme Court victory, African Americans grew more assertive in demanding equal rights. One historic demonstration of this took place on a cold December day in 1955 in Montgomery, Alabama, when seamstress Rosa Parks refused to give up her bus seat to a white man. At that time, public buses in the South were segregated, and African Americans had to ride at the back of the bus and give up their seats to white people. Parks was arrested.

Parks was not the first black person to be arrested for breaking segregation laws. But this time, the local blacks responded by organizing a boycott—a coordinated action by a group of people to stop using or buying something in order to produce a change. The leaders of the Montgomery bus boycott included Dr. Martin Luther King Jr., a young Baptist minister who had recently moved to Montgomery.

The boycott lasted for more than a year. It had a severe economic impact on the bus company and downtown merchants since four out of five of the people who rode the buses were black. More important, it changed the United States forever. By order of the Supreme Court in December 1956, buses were desegregated in Montgomery and blacks were allowed to sit wherever they chose.

The Montgomery bus boycott was inspired by the philosophy of nonviolence—peaceful methods of protesting unfair practices. The philosophy of nonviolence was a defining feature of the civil rights

Rosa Parks *(center)*, accompanied by her lawyer, Charles D. Langford *(right)*, is being led to jail on February 22, 1956, by an unidentified sheriff's deputy after being arrested for participating in the illegal Montgomery bus boycott. The boycott itself was sparked by Parks's arrest three months earlier for refusing to yield her seat to a white man.

movement. It was a test of patience. Even as white crowds grew increasingly violent, protesters were trained to remain peaceful and courteous.

Meanwhile, the vicious activities of the Ku Klux Klan (KKK) increased. The KKK is an organization of white people who once terrorized blacks; bombed churches; and beat and murdered those who opposed its racist beliefs, including whites who participated in the protests.

On February 1, 1960, four students from a black college sat down at the Woolworth's lunch counter in Greensboro, North

Hooded members of the Ku Klux Klan address obviously tense black residents of Lakeland, Florida, on September 1, 1938. For many years beginning in the late 1860s, the Klan, which preached white supremacy, was a menacing presence in African American life. Its members, who often included prominent members of society, terrorized blacks with violent threats, beatings, murder, arson, and bombings.

Carolina. The waitress refused to serve them coffee unless they stood up because only whites were allowed to sit at the counter. The black students stayed in their seats until the store closed. The next day, they returned with more students and the peaceful protest called a sit-in was begun. Across the South, sit-ins by students took place in more than 100 cities in 1960. Although the protesters were persecuted, beaten, and sometimes sent to jail, they continued the peaceful sit-ins until they were served.

A year later, the freedom rides began. People came from all over the country to join demonstrations in the South that peacefully opposed segregation. As they traveled by bus into the South, black and white freedom riders sat together. African Americans were still sitting in the backs of buses in many places in the South and were

Four African American college students stage a sit-in protest at a whites-only lunch counter in Greensboro, North Carolina. Note that the food server is also African American: He was not allowed to eat in the restaurant in which he worked. In many instances in the segregated South, it was okay for blacks to be in the company of whites, so long as the blacks were there to serve whites.

not permitted to use "whites only" restrooms in the terminals. But the freedom riders refused to obey all segregation laws.

In May 1961, the first group of thirteen freedom riders left Washington, D.C., in two buses. The first bus was attacked in both Anniston and Birmingham, Alabama, and the freedom riders were beaten by men with pipes. The second bus was firebombed just outside of Anniston. The freedom riders, not the white mobs, were arrested for "breaking the peace."

Justice was a long time in coming for African Americans. In September 1963, when a bomb exploded during Sunday school at

Smoke billows from this Greyhound bus in Anniston, Alabama, after it was set afire by a mob of white men on May 14, 1961. The bus was carrying a group of freedom riders, sponsored by the Congress of Racial Equality to test the reach of a 1946 Supreme Court decision that outlawed segregated seating of passengers traveling between states.

Birmingham's Sixteenth Street Baptist Church, four girls were killed in the blast. The white men who were known to have set off the bomb weren't arrested. It wasn't until May 2002—nearly forty years later—that a jury found seventy-one-year-old Bobby Frank Cherry guilty. Cherry was a Ku Klux Klan member at the time and was the only surviving defendant.

CHAPTER TWO

The Civil Rights Act and the Civil Rights Movement

The Civil Rights Act of 1964 is a broad law that deals with discrimination in the workplace, voting booths, public accommodations, and educational institutions. It prohibits discrimination by businesses and employers based on race, color, national origin, sex, or religion. It also authorizes the attorney general to file lawsuits to protect constitutional rights in public facilities and public education. The law also extended the Commission on Civil Rights and the Justice Department's Division of Civil Rights, and led to the creation of the Equal Employment Opportunity Commission.

PROVISIONS OF THE CIVIL RIGHTS ACT

The Civil Rights Act consists of ten titles that outline the rights the act granted, and how those rights would be protected. Within these titles, there are numerous sections explaining the law.

Title I deals with voting rights in federal elections for Congress, Senate, and the presidency. Before the law's passage, many Southern states had laws that made it difficult or impossible for blacks to vote in elections. They required voters to pay a poll tax every year, which many African Americans could not afford. Literacy tests required voters to read a section of the state constitution and explain it to the county clerk. This official, who was always white, decided whether a person was literate or not. Title I established that as long as a person is mentally competent and has completed a sixth-grade education, he or she can vote.

Unfortunately this provision did not address state and local elections, leaving a huge loophole for continued voter discrimination. In state and local elections, Southern states could continue using poll taxes and other tactics to keep blacks away from voting booths.

Title II is considered the heart of the Civil Rights Act because it deals with public places. It made it illegal to bar minorities from public facilities, which are defined as inns, hotels, motels, restaurants, retail establishments, gasoline stations, theaters, concert halls, stadiums, or other places of exhibition or entertainment.

Title III authorizes the attorney general to file charges in civil court against anyone who violates the Civil Rights Act and segregates racial minorities. The attorney general was the only one who had the power to enforce the act until 1972, when Congress gave the Equal Employment Opportunity Commission the right to sue companies that discriminate against their employees. Title IX allows the attorney general to take on a discrimination case at the state level.

Title IV deals with the desegregation of all public schools. Students are to be assigned to schools regardless of their race, color, religion, or national origin. The title commissioned a report to determine whether there were adequate schools for all children. It also authorized grants to pay the cost of training for teachers and other school personnel on how to deal with desegregation.

Title V created the Commission on Civil Rights, which is responsible for investigating complaints made by people who are prevented from voting. The commission is also authorized to investigate groups that refuse members because of their color, race, religion, or national origin. Groups are defined as any fraternal organization, college fraternity or sorority, private club, or religious organization.

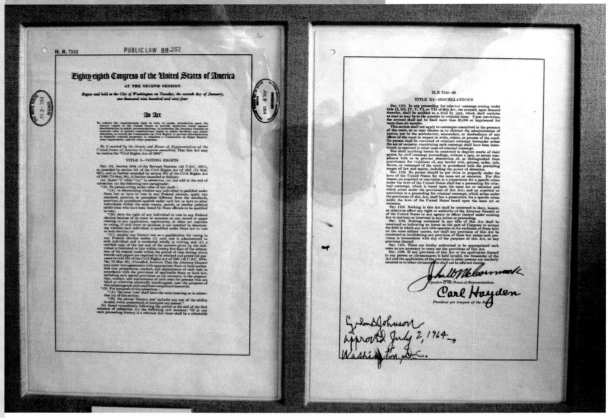

This is the actual Title VII of the Civil Rights Act of 1964, as approved by President Lyndon B. Johnson on July 2, 1964. It is shown here on display at the White House. This section of the law addresses workplace discrimination.

Title VI prohibits discrimination in giving grants and in programs sponsored by the federal government. Many government programs were created under this act. Medicare helps elderly people pay their hospital bills. Medicaid helps those in need afford medical care. Headstart helps young children prepare for kindergarten. The Job Corps finds work for school dropouts. The Teacher Corps trains schoolteachers.

Title VII is one of the most important parts of the Civil Rights Act because it prohibits discrimination in the workplace. An employer or a labor organization cannot legally refuse to hire someone based on his or her race, color, religion, sex, or national

Voting Rights Act Followed by Riots

The outpouring of outrage over violence against blacks led to the passage of the Voting Rights Act of 1965, granting all citizens the right to vote regardless of their literacy or financial status. Yet shortly after the signing of the Voting Rights Act, a six-day riot erupted in Watts, a black neighborhood of Los Angeles, California. It started when a crowd of bystanders argued with police who were about to arrest a young black man. Unfortunately, during the riot, black protesters destroyed their own neighborhood, leaving 34 people dead, 900 injured, and more than $200 million in property damage.

origin. This is the key section for women's rights because it prohibits discrimination against women in the workplace. All salaries, conditions, and perks have to be the same for everyone. Title VII also created the Equal Employment Opportunity Commission to investigate complaints about discrimination in the workplace.

Titles VIII and X authorize the secretary of commerce to conduct a survey for the purpose of compiling registration and voting statistics. Title VIII also established a Community Relations Service as a part of the Department of Commerce.

AFTER THE CIVIL RIGHTS ACT OF 1964

Many leaders in the civil rights movement weren't satisfied by the Civil Rights Act of 1964. They wanted more. They wanted to be able to vote in all elections. When blacks tried to register to vote in the Southern states, they were likely to be attacked or lose their jobs. When this bill passed, only two-fifths of the South's eligible black population was registered to vote.

In Selma, Alabama, voting rights became the focus of a series of marches, starting with more than 100 black teachers. On February 1, 1965, Dr. Martin Luther King Jr. marched to the courthouse with 250 citizens who wanted to register to vote. They were all thrown in

Dr. Martin Luther King Jr. marches with his wife and other civil rights activists through a neighborhood in Selma, Alabama, on his way to Montgomery on March 21, 1965. By this time, King was so popular among African Americans and white supporters of civil rights that almost any event in which he was involved was sure to draw a huge following. Nevertheless, there were many blacks who were impatient with his nonviolent approach.

jail, including King. In protest, more than 500 schoolchildren marched to the courthouse, and they were arrested, too. Two days later, 300 more children were arrested for marching.

Less than a year after the passage of the Civil Rights Act of 1964, a group of 600 people gathered for a march from Selma to the state capitol in Montgomery to support voter registration for blacks. On March 7, the marchers came face-to-face with the sheriff and more than fifty state troopers armed with heavy nightsticks, whips, and gas masks. When the marchers refused to turn back, the troopers advanced and began beating them. One hundred and fifty of the marchers were wounded, and fifty of them were hurt seriously enough to require going to a hospital. Television stations across the United States interrupted their programming to show scenes of policemen on horseback clubbing peaceful marchers.

To protest these attacks by the public authorities, Dr. King led a ministers' march from Selma to Montgomery, starting on March 21, 1965. They started out with more than 2,000 marchers. President Johnson sent 3,000 federal troops and helicopters to protect the marchers on their five-day walk. They entered Montgomery on March 25, with nearly 25,000 people. Governor George Wallace could see the marchers gathered in the capitol from his office, but he refused to accept their petition for voting rights.

In response to the violence inflicted on peaceful protesters, more militant activists began to appear alongside participants of the nonviolent civil rights movement. Some felt the Southern Christian Leadership Conference (SCLC) and the NAACP were not doing enough to stop the authorities from beating and jailing activists. A growing minority of young blacks started fighting back when they were attacked. This younger generation was also proud of being black, and they demanded respect from whites.

The idea of "black power" was proclaimed by the Nation of Islam. Malcolm X was one of its most charismatic leaders, but he was assassinated in 1965 after he broke with the Nation of Islam.

Civil rights leader Malcolm X, pictured here addressing a rally on May 14, 1963, in Harlem, New York, favored a more aggressive approach to fighting racial discrimination than did Martin Luther King Jr. He advocated African American self-government rather than emphasizing equality with whites.

Malcolm X spoke about achieving equality and justice by being strong, independent, and living separately. In Selma during the marches, Malcolm X declared, "White people should thank Dr. King for holding people in check, for there are others who do not believe in these measures."

Over the next two years, there were riots in more than 100 American cities. The Black Panther Party formed in 1966 in Oakland, California, proclaiming its members' right to own and carry weapons to defend themselves against police harassment. Most mainstream newspaper and television coverage emphasized the Black Panthers' violence, paying little attention to the help they gave communities by creating free breakfast programs for kids and clothing for the poor.

Students give the black power salute and cite slogans of racial uplift at a Black Panther liberation school in San Francisco, California, on December 20, 1969. The Black Panther Party was tremendously concerned with the identity of the African American community. Accordingly, it sponsored and supported social programs, such as liberation schools, that emphasized black pride.

A feeling of black pride flooded the nation, and slogans like "Black is beautiful" began to appear. In celebration of their heritage, many African Americans stopped straightening or cutting short their hair, and began to wear it in a natural style called an Afro.

By 1970, more than three-fourths of black Americans lived in cities instead of the rural South. The quest for civil rights moved out of the South and into the rest of the country.

Segregation in housing was an ongoing problem even in the Northern states. Black people often couldn't live outside crowded slums that were run-down and impoverished. In particular, Chicago

Dr. Martin Luther King Jr. stumbles to his knees after being hit by a rock during a march to protest housing discrimination in Chicago on August 5, 1966. King, who continued to lead the march after being injured, always encouraged his followers to remain peaceful and dignified in the face of violent opposition.

was called "the most residentially segregated large city in the nation" in a 1959 report by the U.S. Civil Rights Commission. Dr. King moved to Chicago in 1966 to lead protests and rallies for black citizens. During one march, 350 people tried to go into a white neighborhood, and a mob of 4,000 threw stones at the marchers. Eventually, the Federal Housing Administration agreed to fund a program to build new housing in Chicago's black neighborhoods as mandated by the Civil Rights Act of 1964.

Other minorities were inspired by the civil rights movement and began protesting for equal rights. Cesar Chavez, a migrant worker, set out to organize farm workers in the California grape fields into a union. The farm workers were mostly Hispanic and had an average family income of about $2,000 per year. In 1965, the farm workers went on a strike known as La Causa—"the cause."

Cesar Chavez's hunger strike brought much publicity and public sympathy to the grievances of the farm workers he represented. After twenty-five days, Chavez *(right)* publicly ended his water-only fast by breaking bread with Senator Robert Kennedy in Delano, California, on March 10, 1968.

As quoted in *All the People*, Chavez said, "The fields are sprayed with poisons. The laws that do exist are not enforced. How long will it be before we take seriously the importance of the workers who harvest the food we eat?"

In 1966, Chavez led a 250-mile (402-kilometer) march from Delano to Sacramento to bring attention to the farm workers' conditions. The nonviolent strike lasted three years. Chavez ended the stalemate by going on a twenty-five-day fast, and growers finally signed contracts with the union. In the end, most California grapes were grown in fields with United Farm Workers labor.

A group of Sioux Indians, led by Fear Forgets *(right)*, participates in a "Liberation Day" ceremony on Alcatraz Island, California, on May 31, 1970. The Native Americans occupied the island for more than a year, demanding that the federal government yield control of the island to them. The takeover is one of the most successful Native American civil rights demonstrations in American history.

Native Americans also protested for their rights. In San Francisco, a group of Native Americans, many of them UCLA students, seized an abandoned federal prison on Alcatraz Island and held it for a year and a half, demanding that the island be returned to Native American control. By 1972, militant activists staged a protest occupation at the Bureau of Indian Affairs in Washington, D.C., and took over a trading post at Wounded Knee, South Dakota, where there had been a massacre of Native Americans in 1890.

At the same time, women were demanding equal pay for equal work. Up until the 1950s, women held separate and unequal roles in

Martin Luther King realized that he was putting his life at risk when he took a leadership role in the civil rights movement. King, who won a Nobel peace prize in 1964 for his nonviolent opposition to racial discrimination in the United States, was eventually assassinated on April 4, 1969. Pictured here is a memorial to King that was erected the following day on the balcony of the Lorraine Motel where he was killed.

the workplace. If they wanted to be brain surgeons, architects, or veterinarians, they couldn't because those professions were for men only. Women were usually relegated to low-paying secretarial or nursing jobs. Women were often fired when they got pregnant.

By the late 1960s, women were picketing and demonstrating for equal job opportunities and access to all-male clubs, restaurants, and schools. Feminists started their own publishing houses, child care centers, health clinics, and food cooperatives. The women's liberation movement had its own radicals who wanted to overthrow society and male-dominated institutions.

The violence within the civil rights movement came to a head in February 1968, when black sanitation workers in Memphis, Tennessee, went on strike to protest unfair treatment. During a period of bad weather, twenty-two black workers had been sent home without pay while white workers were paid. On several occasions, Dr. King came to Memphis to speak and help the protesters.

On April 3, King returned to Memphis to lead a march on behalf of the striking workers. He was assassinated the following day as he stood on a balcony of the Lorraine Motel. Though King was dedicated to nonviolence, his own death set off riots in 130 cities across the country. Fires raged in business districts, which were destroyed by looters and arsonists. Sixty-five thousand troops had to be called in to put down the riots. Decades later, black neighborhoods in some cities still have not recovered from these riots.

Because of the riots, many Americans turned away from the civil rights movement and focused on the Vietnam War (1955–1975) instead. But the demonstrations, both nonviolent and militant, had accomplished their goal. Segregation had been declared unlawful, and new opportunities were increasingly being provided for minorities.

CHAPTER THREE

Enforcing the Civil Rights Act of 1964

The U.S. attorney general was authorized to file civil charges against anyone who violated the Civil Rights Act of 1964. Since the passage of the law, the Civil Rights Division of the Department of Justice grew rapidly. Today, the division has more than 350 lawyers working to enforce civil rights laws prohibiting discrimination on the basis of race, sex, disabilities, religion, age, and national origin.

The Civil Rights Act of 1964 was amended and expanded by a series of laws over the years. The division also enforces the Voting Rights Act of 1965, the Equal Credit Opportunity Act, the Americans with Disabilities Act, the National Voter Registration Act, the Age Discrimination in Employment Act, and the Voting Accessibility for the Elderly and Handicapped Act.

It wasn't until the passage of the later acts that other federal departments were granted enforcement ability. For example, in 1988, Congress added an amendment to the Fair Housing Act that allowed the Departments of Justice and Housing and Urban Development to enforce the law.

The courts also play an important role in interpreting the law and upholding civil rights. Federal courts serve as a check on state and local discrimination, while a single Supreme Court ruling can change the way a minority group is treated throughout the country.

THE EQUAL EMPLOYMENT OPPORTUNITY COMMISSION (EEOC)

The Equal Employment Opportunity Commission (EEOC) was created by the Civil Rights Act of 1964 (under Title VII) to eliminate discrimination from the workplace. Yet, at first, the EEOC had no law enforcement ability. It could only mediate, or act as a go-between, to create agreements between employers and employees.

The EEOC created a clearinghouse of information about workplace discrimination based on race, color, religion, sex, or national origin. Only when the EEOC found "patterns or practices" of discrimination could it refer cases to the Department of Justice for litigation.

Based on its research, the EEOC recommended federal laws and policies to the president and Congress. It also issued public service announcements and educated employers to prevent discrimination.

The EEOC started out with a backlog of nearly 1,000 complaints, called charges. In the first year alone, 8,852 charges were filed.

The majority of the EEOC's work during the 1960s involved race discrimination. One early agreement was negotiated with the Newport News Shipbuilding and Drydock Company. Five thousand black employees were finally desegregated in company bathrooms and lunchrooms. They obtained equal pay for performing the same jobs as white workers and were able to attend apprenticeship programs and compete for supervisory jobs.

Yet from the very beginning, one-third of the complaints were about sex discrimination. The EEOC insisted that employers could not have different hiring policies for women because they were married or had young children, unless they had the same policy for men. Work also couldn't be classified as "light" or "heavy." This allowed more women to begin working in formerly all-male, blue-collar jobs that paid much better than being a waitress or cashier.

A milestone for the EEOC was its investigation of four of the United States' largest employers in 1973: General Electric, General Motors, Ford, and Sears Roebuck. The EEOC negotiated settlements, including one for $29.4 million in back pay and benefits for minority and female workers.

One year after the EEOC began operations, it issued Guidelines on Religious Discrimination. These guidelines required employers to make reasonable accommodations for the religious practices of employees. Also in 1966, the EEOC issued Guidelines on Employment Testing Procedures, stating that racial groups could not be tested differently.

In 1970, the EEOC issued Guidelines on National Origin Discrimination, outlawing requirements such as certain language skills, and height and weight standards. Some people had even been turned down for jobs because they had foreign-sounding surnames.

Congress conducted public hearings on employment discrimi- nation in 1971 to see what effect the Civil Rights Act of 1964 was having in the United States. It concluded there was still a lot of discrimination in the workplace and that blacks, Hispanics, and women were in the lowest-paid positions and in the lowest-paid industries.

Based on these findings, Congress finally gave the EEOC law enforcement ability in the Equal Employment Opportunity Act of 1972. Now the EEOC could sue those who violated the Civil Rights Act. This gave the EEOC a lot more power in its negotiations with employers.

JUDICIAL DECISIONS

The first court challenge of the Civil Rights Act of 1964 came almost as soon as it was passed. Many wondered if the Supreme Court would rule the act unconstitutional—denying that Congress had the power to make segregation illegal under the Fourteenth

Discriminating Against Older Americans

The Age Discrimination in Employment Act was passed in 1967, and the first EEOC lawsuit based on age discrimination was against the Leo Burnett Company. The company agreed to pay $375,000 in back pay to seventeen former employees and to provide pension adjustments because the advertising agency had forced its employees to retire at age sixty-two. By the 1980s, age discrimination became an important focus for the EEOC because many corporations were downsizing—employees were laid off in order to streamline company expenses—and older workers were often the first to go.

Amendment. But the Supreme Court unanimously upheld the Civil Rights Act of 1964.

The Supreme Court justices decided several cases in the 1970s that supported the EEOC's broad definition of discrimination and its suggestions for how to eliminate it. The most cited case in employment discrimination law was *McDonnell Douglas Corp v. Green* (1973), in which the Supreme Court decided how to determine whether a worker was not hired because of discrimination. If an employer rejected a qualified minority worker but continued to look for or hired a worker with similar qualifications, the employer was guilty of discrimination.

Native Americans also won in court because of the Civil Rights Act of 1964. Their rights granted in treaties, some 100 years old, were finally confirmed. In 1971, Aleuts, Inuits, and other native Alaskans were awarded 40 million acres (16.2 million hectares) of land and nearly $1 billion in settlement. In Maine, Penobscot Indians received $81 million for claims based on a law passed in 1790.

For women, workplace discrimination was still severe. From 1959 to 1981, women's earnings actually fell from 64 percent of men's salaries, down to 59 percent of men's salaries. Eighty percent of all women workers were employed in the lowest-paying 5 percent of jobs.

At the Minnesota Mining and Manufacturing Company, women were discriminated against in job assignments, wages, promotions,

President Richard Nixon *(second from right)* discusses a proposal to settle claims by Native Americans in Alaska with Donald R. Wright *(right)*, president of the Alaska Federation of Natives, at a meeting at the White House on April 6, 1971. Looking on are Alaska senator Ted Stevens *(left)* and Secretary of the Interior Rogers Morton. Nixon proposed giving the Native Americans 40 million acres of land (16 million hectares) and 1 billion dollars. During his presidency, he proposed several pieces of legislation aimed at boosting economic development, tribal self-rule, and cultural awareness in Native American communities.

and transfers. The EEOC reached a settlement with the company in 1982 on six lawsuits. The settlement required elimination of unfair practices and provided $2.3 million to 2,350 women.

The courts also supported the EEOC when it issued Guidelines on Sexual Harassment in 1980. The EEOC determined that a "hostile work environment" is one in which unwelcome sexual conduct affects the environment of the workplace. The EEOC prohibited employers and supervisors from demanding sexual favors from workers.

Major Civil Rights Legislation and Court Decisions

1863 Emancipation Proclamation is issued, freeing slaves.

1866 Civil Rights Act of 1866.

1868 Fourteenth Amendment passes, granting citizenship to everyone born in the United States.

1869 Fifteenth Amendment passes, granting all citizens the right to vote.

1896 Supreme Court decision *Plessy v. Ferguson* creates doctrine of "separate but equal."

1954 Supreme Court decision *Brown v. Board of Education* abolishes segregation in public schools.

1956 Supreme Court decides segregation on buses in Montgomery, Alabama, is illegal.

1957 Civil Rights Act of 1957 establishes the Civil Rights Division of the U.S. Department of Justice.

1960 Supreme Court bans segregation in bus terminals.

1964 Twenty-fourth Amendment to the Constitution outlaws poll taxes in federal elections.

1964 Civil Rights Act of 1964 abolishes segregation and discrimination in the workplace.

1965 Voting Rights Act grants the right to vote to all citizens in local, state, and federal elections.

Early in the 1990s, Congress passed the Americans with Disabilities Act, the Older Workers Benefit Protection Act, and the Civil Rights Act of 1991. The Civil Rights Act of 1991 gave people the right to a jury trial in discrimination cases and also set a limit of $300,000 that could be awarded for damages.

The Americans with Disabilities Act of 1990 (ADA) made it illegal to discriminate against people with disabilities. People with disabilities couldn't be denied services, jobs, benefits, or public activities. Since 43 million Americans have one or more physical or mental disabilities, this act benefits a lot of people.

Before the ADA, deaf people couldn't talk to 911 operators if they had an emergency. Now, all emergency services have telephone

President George H. W. Bush signs the Americans with Disabilities Act into law during a ceremony at the White House on July 26, 1990. In his remarks at the ceremony, the president said that the law would give disabled Americans "the opportunity to blend fully and equally into the rich mosaic of the American mainstream."

devices for the deaf (TDD). For people in wheelchairs, a flight of steps used to keep them out of most government and public buildings. Now, wheelchair ramps are required so all citizens have equal access.

CONCLUSION

The civil rights movement in the United States was the beginning of a powerful revolution in how human beings should be treated. A single standard of equality and fairness was demanded for everyone. It was an important milestone in the march ever onward toward a better world.

Congressman John Lewis *(center)* of Georgia marks the fortieth anniversary of the Selma-to-Montgomery march by crossing Alabama's Edmund Pettus Bridge with other members of Congress on March 6, 2005. Lewis was one of the leaders of the original march with Dr. Martin Luther King. He also led a number of sit-ins during the 1960s and was one of the main speakers at the March on Washington in 1963. He continues to champion civil rights issues.

Unfortunately, discrimination today is still a very serious problem. The EEOC continues to receive complaints in record numbers. Race discrimination has increased every single decade since the Civil Rights Act was passed in 1964. Women still make only seventy-five cents for every dollar a man earns in the same job. Sexual harassment complaints almost tripled in the 1990s compared to the 1980s. The EEOC is also receiving record numbers of complaints of discrimination based on age and disability. And nearly 20 percent of all cases are about retaliation against employees who complain about discrimination.

The hard work, idealism, and commitment of civil rights activists have changed the world, but it is every American's responsibility to make sure that people are treated equally. That is the only way to create a better world for everyone.

GLOSSARY

assassin Someone who kills an important person for political or ideological reasons.

bill A proposed law.

boycott A coordinated action by a group of people to stop using or buying something in order to produce a change.

civil rights Individual rights that all members of a society have to freedom and equal treatment under the law.

desegregate To do away with the practice of separating people of different races in schools, restaurants, and other public places.

discriminate To treat people differently than others simply because of their race, national origin, sex, or religion.

downsize To lay off employees in order to streamline company expenses.

ethnic group A section of the population that is identified by race, national origin, religion, or other distinctive cultural traits.

filibuster A tactic used to delay or prevent a vote on a bill in the Senate by engaging in long speeches and debates.

lynching Public murder that is often racially motivated.

nonviolence Peaceful methods of protesting inequalities in society.

poll tax A tax or fee that a person is required to pay to be eligible to vote.

prejudice An irrational bias against someone or a group based on race, national origin, religion, sex, or other trait.

segregation The practice of separating people of different races in schools, restaurants, and other public places.

sit-in A peaceful protest in which people refuse to leave "white-only" establishments until they are served.

the South The Southern states in the United States that allowed slavery and fought on the Confederate side of the Civil War.

FOR MORE INFORMATION

U.S. Department of Justice
Civil Rights Division
950 Pennsylvania Avenue NW
Washington, DC 20530
(202) 514-4609
Web site: http://www.usdoj.gov/crt/crt-home.html
The Civil Rights Division of the Department of Justice is responsible
for enforcing federal statutes prohibiting discrimination on the basis
of race, sex, handicap, religion, and national origin.

Equal Employment Opportunity Commission (EEOC)
1801 L Street NW
Washington, DC 20507
(202) 663-4900
TTD: (202) 663-4494
Web site: http://www.eeoc.gov
The EEOC is a federal agency that focuses on eliminating illegal
discrimination from the workplace.

U.S. Commission on Civil Rights
624 Ninth Street NW
Washington, DC 20425
(202) 376-8128
Web site: http://www.usccr.gov
The commission performs fact-finding and investigates complaints
of civil rights violations and refers them to the appropriate federal,
state, or local government agency or private organization for action.

Web Sites

Due to the changing nature of Internet links, the Rosen Publishing Group, Inc., has developed an online list of Web sites related to the subject of this book. This site is updated regularly. Please use this link to access the list:

http://www.rosenlinks.com/lallp/cira

FOR FURTHER READING

Bolden, Tonya. *Tell All the Children Our Story: Memories and Mementos of Being Young and Black in America.* New York, NY: Henry A. Abrams, 2002.

Carter, Jimmy. *An Hour Before Daylight: Memories of a Rural Boyhood.* New York, NY: Simon & Schuster, 2001.

Chafe, William Henry, et al., eds. *Remembering Jim Crow: African Americans Tell About Life in the Segregated South.* New York, NY: The New Press, 2001.

Crowe, Chris. *Getting Away with Murder: The True Story of the Emmett Till Case.* New York, NY: Penguin Young Readers Group, 2003.

George, Linda, and Charles George. *Civil Rights Marches.* New York, NY: Children's Press, 1999.

King, Casey, and Barrett Osborne. *Oh, Freedom!* New York, NY: Alfred A. Knopf, 1997.

Levine, Ellen, ed. *Freedom's Children: Young Civil Rights Activists Tell Their Own Stories.* New York, NY: G. P. Putnam, 1993.

Santiago, Esmeralda. *When I Was a Puerto Rican.* New York, NY: Vintage, 1993.

Wexler, Sanford. *The Civil Rights Movement: An Eyewitness History.* New York, NY: Facts on File, 1993.

Williams, Juan. *Eyes on the Prize: America's Civil Rights Years, 1954–1965.* New York, NY: Viking, 1987.

BIBLIOGRAPHY

Carson, Clayborne, et al., eds. *The Eyes on the Prize Civil Rights Reader: Documents, Speeches and Firsthand Accounts from the Black Freedom Struggle, 1954–1990.* New York, NY: Penguin Books, 1991.

Crowe, Chris. *Getting Away with Murder: The True Story of the Emmett Till Case.* New York, NY: Penguin Young Readers Group, 2003.

Davis, Townsend. *Weary Feet, Rested Souls: A Guided History of the Civil Rights Movement.* New York, NY: W. W. Norton and Company, 1998.

Hakim, Joy. *All the People: 1945–2001.* New York, NY: Oxford University Press, 2003.

Hampton, Henry, et al., eds. *Voices of Freedom: An Oral History of the Civil Rights Movement from the 1950s Through the 1980s.* New York, NY: Bantam, 1990.

Kull, Andrew. *The Color-Blind Constitution.* Cambridge, MA: Harvard University Press, 1992.

Lyon, Danny. *Memories of the Southern Civil Rights Movement.* Chapel Hill, NC: University of North Carolina Press, 1993.

Powledge, Fred. *We Shall Overcome: Heroes of the Civil Rights Movement.* New York, NY: Charles Scribner's Sons, 1993.

Sitkoff, Harvard. *The Struggle for Black Equality, 1954–1992.* New York, NY: Hill and Wang, 1993.

Weisbrot, Robert. *Freedom-Bound: A History of America's Civil Rights Movement.* New York, NY: W. W. Norton and Company, 1990.

White, John. *Black Leadership in America, 1895–1968.* New York, NY: Longman, 1985.

INDEX

J

Jim Crow laws, 10–12
Job Corps, 22
Johnson, President Lyndon B., 6–8, 25

K

Kennedy, President John F., 5–6
King, Dr. Martin Luther, Jr., 6, 15, 23, 25,
    26, 28, 32
  assassination of, 32
Ku Klux Klan (KKK), 16, 19

L

Lincoln, President Abraham, 9
literacy tests, 20–21
Little Rock, Arkansas, 15
Lum, Gong, 11
lynchings, 12

M

Malcolm X, 25–26
march(es), 4, 25, 29, 32
March on Washington, 6
Marshall, Thurgood, 13
McDonnell Douglas Corp v. Green, 36
Minnesota Mining and Manufacturing
    Company, 36
Montgomery bus boycott, 15

N

National Association for the
    Advancement of Colored People
    (NAACP), 12–13, 25
National Voter Registration Act, 33
Nation of Islam, 25
Native Americans, 12, 30, 36
Newport News Shipbuilding and Drydock
    Company, 34

O

Older Workers Benefit Protection Act, 38

P

Parks, Rosa, 15
Plessy, Homer, 10
poll tax, 20, 21, 38

S

segregation, 4, 6, 9, 12, 18, 32, 35
Senate, 8, 20
"separate but equal" doctrine, 10, 13
sit-ins, 4, 17
Sixteenth Street Baptist Church, bombing
    of, 18–19
slavery, 9–10
Smith, Congressman Howard, 8
Southern Christian Leadership Conference
    (SCLC), 25
St. George, Congresswoman Katherine, 8

T

Teacher Corps, 22
Till, Emmett, 4
Truman, President Harry S., 12

U

United Farm Workers, 29
U.S. Civil Rights Commission, 28
U.S. Supreme Court, 10–11, 13, 15, 33,
    35–36, 38

V

Vietnam War, 32
Voting Accessibility for the Elderly and
    Handicapped Act, 33
Voting Rights Act of 1965, 23, 33, 38

W

Wallace, Governor George, 25
Warren, Chief Justice Earl, 13
women's liberation movement, 30–31
women's rights, 8, 23
World War II, 12–13

About the Author

Susan Wright is a writer living in New York City. She has written books and interactive workbooks on science and popular culture. She comes to this project with an intense interest in civil rights movements all over the world. She attended her first civil rights march in 1993.

Photo Credits

Cover, p. 1 © Royalty Free/Corbis; pp. 5, 14 (top, bottom left), 16, 17, 18, 19, 26, 27, 28, 29, 30, 37 © Bettmann/Corbis; p. 7 © AFP/Getty Images, Inc.; p. 11 © Getty Images, Inc.; p. 14 (bottom right) © Phil Schermeister/Corbis; p. 22 © Mannie Garcia/Reuters/Corbis; pp. 24, 31 © Flip Schulke/Corbis; pp. 39, 40 © AP/Wide World Photos.

Designer: Thomas Forget; Editor: Wayne Anderson